# CAN SCIENCE SOLVE?

## THE MYSTERY OF
# HAUNTED HOUSES

## Chris Oxlade

Heinemann
LIBRARY

**www.heinemann.co.uk/library**
Visit our website to find out more information about Heinemann Library books.

To order:
 Phone 44 (0) 1865 888112
Send a fax to 44 (0) 1865 314091
 Visit the Heinemann Bookshop at www.heinemann.co.uk/library to browse our
catalogue and order online.

First published in Great Britain by Heinemann Library, Halley
Court, Jordan Hill, Oxford OX2 8EJ, part of Harcourt Education.
Heinemann is a registered trademark of Harcourt Education Ltd.

Editorial: Clare Lewis
Design: Victoria Bevan and Q2A
Production: Helen McCreath

Printed in China

10 digit ISBN 0 431 01891 X
13 digit ISBN 978 0 431 01891 1
10 09 08 07 06
10 9 8 7 6 5 4 3 2 1

**British Library Cataloguing in Publication Data**
Oxlade, Chris
Can Science Solve: The Mystery of Haunted Houses – 2nd edition
133.122
A full catalogue record for this book is available from the British
Library.

**Acknowledgements**
The publishers would like to thank the following for permission
to reproduce photographs:
James David Travel Photography: p11 (lower); Mary Evans
Picture Library: pp6, 11 (upper), 15; FLPA: Silvestris p19; Fortean
Picture Library: pp8, 9, 27, A Hart-David p22, M Jackson p28,
G Lyon Playfair p21, A Trottmann p25, T Vaci p24; Ronald Grant
Archive: p7; Marsden Archive: S Marsden pp4, 29; Thames Water:
p17; Trip: M Peters p20; Ultra Photos: Y Nixiteas p23; Stewart
Weir: pp13, 14.

Cover photograph reproduced with permission of Getty/
National Geographic.

The publishers would like to thank Sarah Williams for her
assistance in the preparation of this book.

Every effort has been made to contact copyright holders of any
material reproduced in this book. Any omissions will be rectified
in subsequent printings if notice is given to the publishers.

The paper used to print this book comes from sustainable
resources.

# CONTENTS

# UNSOLVED MYSTERIES

For hundreds of years, people have been interested in and puzzled by mysterious places, creatures and events. What secrets does a black hole hold? Does the Abominable Snowman actually exist? Why do ships and planes vanish without trace when they cross the Bermuda Triangle? Are some houses really haunted by ghosts? These mysteries have baffled scientists, who have spent years trying to find the answers. But just how far can science go? Can it really explain the seemingly unexplainable? Or are there some mysteries which science simply cannot solve? Read on, and make your own mind up...

This book tells you about haunted houses and the ghosts in them. It retells eyewitness accounts. It looks at the possible scientific explanations for the experiences of the eyewitnesses, and examines how to investigate a haunting.

Glamis Castle in Scotland is said to be haunted by many ghosts, including Macbeth, a medieval king. But ghosts turn up in normal houses too.

## What is a haunted house?

A ghost is said to be the soul of a dead person which returns to the world of the living. It shows its presence by appearing as a figure or a light of some kind, by making strange noises, such as clanking and laughter, or by making objects move about. A haunted house is a place where the same ghost keeps appearing, or where there are a series of ghostly events. In a haunted house, many of the ghosts that appear are in the likeness of previous occupants of the house, often ones who have met a hideous death!

It's not just houses, castles and **stately homes** which are haunted. Any building can have a ghost – prisons, theatres, hotels, public houses and even factories.

Many stories of hauntings are made up, and many ghost sightings are just imagined, but there are still many cases where reliable witnesses have seen a ghost that has no explanation. Is there anything science can do to solve this peculiar mystery?

# BEGINNINGS OF A MYSTERY

It is impossible to say when people first started seeing ghosts, but it must have been many thousands of years ago. Since very ancient times, people have believed that a person's spirit can exist separately from his or her body, and that when he or she dies, the spirit lives on in some way.

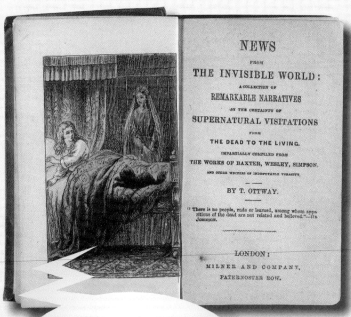

Ghost and other paranormal stories were popular in Victorian times, as shown by this book published in about 1850.

Ghost stories are common in **folklore**, but most are fiction, and exaggerated to make them as scary as possible. Over the last few hundred years, many old houses have gained a reputation for being haunted by the ghosts of people who died in them, or on the spot where they were built. The first proper investigations into hauntings were made in the 19th century.

## More apparitions

Not all apparitions are haunting apparitions. Some are apparitions of the living, where people who are still alive appear to be in two places at the same time. 'Crisis' apparitions have appeared when a living person dies or is involved in an accident, normally to a friend or relative of that person, who is in a completely different place. Some apparitions are not hauntings, because they appear only once.

## Types of ghost

When you think of a ghost, you probably think of a Hollywood movie ghost – a **transparent** figure dressed in white, floating through the walls of an old country house, and making strange moaning noises! In fact, there are very few sightings of ghosts like this.

A ghost can be in the form of an **apparition**, which is a visible figure of a person. An apparition might look solid or see-through, float through the air or walk. Apparitions are not always of people – they are sometimes of animals or monsters. The apparition can be accompanied by noises.

Not all hauntings involve an apparition. Often there are just noises such as laughter, music, footsteps, groaning and whistling, and some hauntings involve objects which appear to move on their own. This sort of ghost is called a poltergeist. A **poltergeist** is normally, but not always, **malicious**, throwing objects across rooms, stones against windows, upsetting furniture and so on. The word 'poltergeist' means noisy spirit.

The apparition of Marley's ghost from the 1970 version of the film Scrooge, with clanking chains for effect!

7

# DID YOU SEE THAT?

There are literally thousands of people who have had ghostly experiences in haunted houses and other buildings. Obviously we cannot look at them all in this book. So on the next four pages, we will look at examples which show the range of experiences people have had in haunted houses. We'll start with an in-depth look at one of the most famous haunted houses ever.

## Borley Rectory

For more than a century, Borley Rectory, a Victorian building in the **county** of Essex, was said to be the most haunted house in England. Borley Rectory was built in 1863, close to Borley Church and on ground where a medieval monastery had once stood.

The Rectory's first residents were the Reverend Henry Bull and his family. Not long after moving in they began to hear footsteps, tapping noises, voices and ringing bells at night. Then ghostly figures began to appear – one child saw an old man in a hat at her bedside and a visitor saw a nun wandering in the corridors.

Borley Rectory, photographed in 1929.

In 1892, Henry Bull's son took over the Rectory, but the strange happenings continued. The residents saw a headless man in the garden and a ghostly coach in the drive. A locked door mysteriously unlocked itself every night. In 1929 the **poltergeists** moved in. Keys and other objects began to appear from nowhere. Later, new occupants heard voices and footsteps, and saw scribbled messages appear on the walls.

The bizarre events continued until 1939, when the Rectory was mysteriously burned to the ground. Witnesses saw dark figures leaving the burning building and a young girl's face looking from one of the upstairs windows, even though there should have been nobody inside.

Some of the scrawled messages which appeared mysteriously on the walls of Borley Rectory (the capital letters were written by investigators).

Eventually, houses were built on the site. Nobody knows the reasons for the hauntings, but during the excavations for the new houses, pendants with religious symbols were found, together with a woman's skull. There is also a theory that the ghosts were of a monk from the former monastery and a nun from a nearby convent, who were killed as they tried to run away together in a coach and horses.

# MORE HAUNTINGS

Here are four other cases of hauntings, which have been chosen to show the wide range of different ghostly experiences which people have had in haunted houses.

## Cornish holiday cottage

In 1947, two women arrived at their holiday cottage, which was an old wooden shack, in Cornwall, England. They unpacked and went to bed. At about 11.30, they heard footsteps and growling outside, followed a few minutes later by the sound of the shack door opening and closing, even though they had bolted the door. Then there were more noises – the sound of footsteps in the living room, the rustling of paper and chuckling laughter. Finally the women opened the bedroom door. They found the living room empty, but the rocking-chair rocking by itself, and there were more sounds of laughter, rustling and the growling of a dog. In the morning the women complained to the owner, who said that other guests had had similar experiences.

## George and Dragon Inn

Inhabitants of the George and Dragon Inn in the town of Chester, England, are said to be able to hear footsteps regularly coming from the upstairs rooms of the building. The steps seem to pace first one way and then, 20 minutes later, back the other way. The building is on the site of a cemetery where Roman soldiers were buried more than 1600 years ago.

The White House, the official residence of the President of the United States, is said to be haunted by the ghost of Abraham Lincoln, who was President from 1861 to 1865.

## Raynham Hall

In 1786, a woman dressed in brown appeared twice in Raynham Hall, Norfolk, England. The first time was to King George III, and the second to a group of men on watch for her. She walked straight through one of them, who felt 'an ice-cold cloud' pass through his bones. The figure appeared in the house several times in 1835, to different people at different times, with 'dark holes' where her eyes should have been. People believe the lady is the ghost of Dorothy Walpole, who married the owner of Raynham Hall, and may have been murdered by him there in 1711.

## Yorkshire house

In the mid 1980s, a teenage girl moved into a 200-year-old house with her father. After a few days, they began to hear bumps and bangs from downstairs, as if the furniture was being moved about. In fact, sometimes it actually did. Objects, such as keys, began to appear and disappear and the lights turned on and off without anybody touching the switches. The girl, now a woman in her twenties, thinks the ghost could be that of the old man who had lived and died in the house before she moved in.

# BUMPS IN THE NIGHT

Most reports of hauntings involve strange noises rather than **apparitions**. The wide range of sounds that witnesses hear includes creaking, bumps, cracks, knocks, sliding noises, groaning, laughter and crying. Can any of these ghostly noises be explained by science?

## Expansion and contraction

All materials expand (get bigger) and contract (get smaller) when their temperature changes. In most cases, they expand as the temperature rises and contract as the temperature falls. The amount that a material expands or contracts is only small. For example, a wooden metre rule would only expand by a fraction of a millimetre if its temperature increased by 1°Centigrade.

Different materials expand and contract at different rates, so the expansion of one material might be greater than the expansion of another if they both undergo the same temperature rise. If two materials which expand and contract at different rates are pressed against each other, then as the temperature rises and falls, they try to move against each other. Because of **friction**, the movement does not happen smoothly, but in a series of little jumps. As each jump happens, the materials vibrate, creating a knocking noise, or a creaking noise if the jumps happen in quick succession.

If you have central heating in your home, you might hear creaking noises as the heating comes on and the pipes and radiators begin to warm up. It is caused by the metal pipes expanding and moving against their fastenings.

Wood does not necessarily have to be in contact with other materials to make creaking noises. Wood is made of millions of fibres lying next to each other, so if some fibres expand before the fibres next to them, creaking noises can result. The expansion can be caused by heating and cooling, but also if the wood becomes damp or dries out. Water makes its way into the fibres and makes them expand. The **water vapour** in damp air is enough to make the outer layers of the wood expand.

An old doorway containing a combination of materials – iron, wood and brick – which expand and contract at different rates.

# WEATHER CHANGES

The changes of temperature and **humidity** which cause building materials to make creaking noises are regularly created by the weather. On a sunny morning, sunshine hits a cold building. Dark parts of the building capture the heat and warm up. At the end of the day, as the Sun goes down and the air cools, so does the building, with the outside parts cooling first. These regular changes, especially the ones at night, can be the cause of ghostly noises. And as the weather patterns or seasons change, with changes of humidity, dry wood can gradually become damp and vice versa.

## Renovations

Alterations and additions to a building also create the conditions which cause its structure and furnishings to creak. For example, putting a central heating system into an old house makes the timbers of the house, which may have been slightly damp for hundreds of years, gradually dry out. Installing new windows and doors, which create new air flows through the house, or uncovering beams to give the house an 'old-world' look, can also cause timbers to dry out.

Houses such as these, built in the Tudor period (1485–1603), have wooden frames, which dry out and creak if modern heating is installed.

Expansion and contraction of new window and door frames can cause not only creaking, but also the windows and doors themselves to jam closed and even to open by themselves.

## Plumbing

Plumbing, especially old plumbing, also causes strange noises. Air trapped in the pipes causes peculiar gurgling noises as the water flows past it. Sound also travels very well along the pipes, so a sound made in one place can seem to come from everywhere in the house. Water hammer, which is caused by shock **waves** bouncing from one end of a pipe to the other if a tap is closed too quickly, creates very loud clanking noises.

So it may not be a coincidence that older houses, which tend to have a wooden framework of columns and beams as well as old plumbing, seem more likely to be haunted by ghostly noises.

Plumbing installed in the 19th century – often a cause of ghostly glugs and gurgles!

# SOUND ON THE MOVE

One reason why noises sound ghostly is that they often seem to come out of thin air. For example, you might hear the sound of talking from an empty room. Many such occurrences can be explained by investigating the way in which sound travels.

## Waves and echoes

Sound is created by any object that vibrates. The vibrations travel away from the object in **waves**. As the sound travels, it gets weaker, so the further a listener is from you, the quieter your voice sounds. When sound hits the boundary between two different materials, it bounces.

In fact, sound does not travel very well in air. It travels much better through solids and liquids. So imagine if a person taps a plumbing pipe in one room of a house. Sound waves go both into the air and into the pipe. In the air, the sound weakens and bounces off the walls. But in the pipe, it travels well through the solid metal, and can be heard clearly in all the other rooms in the house where the plumbing goes. The same thing happens with solid walls and floors – sound travels easily from room to room and even from house to house.

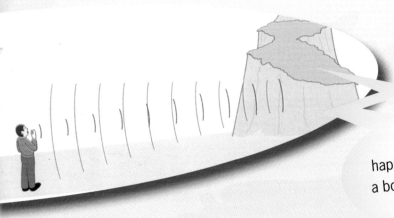

Ghostly echoes happen when sound reaches a boundary in materials, such as the air and rock.

## Sounds under the ground

Underground mine shafts and tunnels may be the cause of haunting effects. Sound travels along them, making sounds from far off seem to come from the ground, and air moves through them, making them behave like a huge musical instrument. Sounds travelling down into the ground, such as footsteps, can also be reflected back up when they hit the tunnels. Other **geological** features, such as the boundary between layers of soft and hard rock, can reflect sound and hidden underground streams and water pipes carry sound well.

## Ground subsidence

**Subsidence** happens when the ground collapses under a building's foundations. It is caused by old mine workings collapsing or soft rocks such as clay drying out in a dry summer. Subsidence is sometimes catastrophic, but normally happens slowly, with the building slowly cracking up. As the ground and foundations move, the house will make creaking and cracking noises without the movements being felt inside.

Underground tunnels, such as this sewer, can cause unusual sounds and echoes.

# NOT WHAT IT SEEMS

We've seen how most ghostly sounds can be explained as creaks and groans made by the houses which are supposed to be haunted. But what can science do to explain **apparitions** and objects moving about on their own?

## Tricks of the light

At night in a spooky house, it's easy to imagine shadows and lights as ghostly figures. But a trick of the light can be the cause. For example, the glass in old windows is never perfectly flat because of the way it was made. Light does not pass straight through, but is **refracted** in different directions, distorting the images of objects on the other side. Simple reflections, even of yourself, in glass doors can also look like ghostly figures because the glass creates a see-through reflection. You don't normally notice these reflections because of the light coming from the other side of the glass.

Light can also be reflected from outside the house. For example, light from car headlights can shine from a long distance through windows and be reflected around, creating ghostly images. On stormy nights, lightning can create similar effects. Outside, especially in marshy ground, small patches of rising mist can look like ghostly figures.

Fog and mist, such as this early morning mist over a lake, can make the shapes of common objects look like ghostly figures.

## Moving objects

The same ground movements which cause houses to **subside** can also cause objects in the house to move around. Gradual, slow movement over a period of days may go unnoticed, but can cause shelves and surfaces to slope slightly. Sometimes the overall movement is enough to make ornaments slide or topple as if they are being moved by an invisible hand.

## Low-frequency noise

The **frequency** of a sound is a measure of how many **waves** pass a point every second. It is measured in hertz. The human ear can detect a wide range of frequencies, but not very high or very low ones. Research has shown that very low-frequency noise (lower than 10 hertz) can cause some people to 'see' objects which are not really there, perhaps because the sound vibrates the eye's **retina** in some way.

# ALL IN THE MIND

**Apparitions** are hard to explain. If the witnesses are reliable, and the apparition cannot be simply explained as a trick of the light, then there seems to be no logical explanation of why they see a ghostly figure. Unless, that is, the apparition is a trick of the mind – a **hallucination** of some sort.

Hallucinations are a recognized medical side-effect. Diseases such as malaria can make people hallucinate, and so can taking certain medicines for treating disease. Of course, we all have hallucinations when we dream, and it's likely that many 'ghosts' simply appear in very realistic dreams. However, simple hallucinations would not seem to explain ghosts that are seen by several people at the same time.

Other theories about hallucinations rely on the existence of extra-sensory perception (ESP). This is where a person somehow receives information in their brain without using their normal five senses to collect it. The theories suggest that the person who sees the ghost actually sees a picture projected into his or her mind by somebody else. Scientific experiments have been carried out to try to show that ESP exists, but none have been conclusive.

Clairvoyants use their natural 'sixth sense', or ESP, to see into the future. Some people are convinced it works; others are sceptical.

## Back from the dead

**Parapsychologists** believe that dead people's spirits live on and can affect living people. The dead people may use ESP to project their presence into a living person's mind, so that the living person sees them, perhaps deliberately, perhaps by mistake. Parapsychologists believe that some people have a natural ability to pick up these signals from the dead, and the signals are from dead people telling the living that death is not the end of life, or that they are refusing to accept their own death.

## Mind over matter

**Telekinesis** is the ability of a person to make objects move without touching them, by mind power alone. Some parapsychologists think that **poltergeists** are spirits using telekinesis. Again, experiments have been carried out to see if telekinesis is possible, such as a person trying to affect the roll of dice, but none have been conclusive.

Uri Geller bending a spoon, apparently by mind power alone. Could the spirits of the dead move objects in a similar way?

# HAUNTED HOUSE INVESTIGATIONS

**To attempt to discover the possible cause of a haunting, it is necessary to carry out a special investigation of the haunted site. Psychic investigators specialize in these investigations. An investigation needs a logical, scientific approach to find the facts of the case, to discover a natural cause if there is one and to rule out other causes.**

## The witnesses

An investigator's first job is to interview the witnesses who have seen or heard anything and to write down, or record on tape, what they say. The interview includes asking questions which attempt to find out what actually happened rather than the witness' interpretation of what happened. For example, the witness may say that he or she heard footsteps. It is up to an investigator to find out what the 'footsteps' really sounded like, because it may have been different to his or her idea of what footsteps sound like. Questions like this can also help the investigator to decide whether the witness' story is reliable, exaggerated or even invented.

Researchers recording ground vibrations caused by underground water movements, which they think could cause objects to move in a 'haunted' house.

The investigator should also ask about the witnesses' health and whether they are taking medicines, because illness and drugs can cause **hallucinations** or affect sight.

## The haunted site

The investigator should also make a close examination of the haunted site. This includes making an accurate plan of the rooms where the witness saw or heard the ghost. The plan should include the positions of the witnesses and the movements of the **apparition** or the direction any sounds appeared to come from. They should also note the position of anything which could affect the light or sound in the rooms, such as windows, mirrors and thin walls. Photos of the rooms can also be taken to go with the plan.

Armed with the statements, recordings, plans, photographs and notes, an investigator can go away and attempt to solve the mystery, perhaps with the help of old maps and books on local history. He or she may be able to suggest a natural cause, such as faulty plumbing, but there will not always be an explanation.

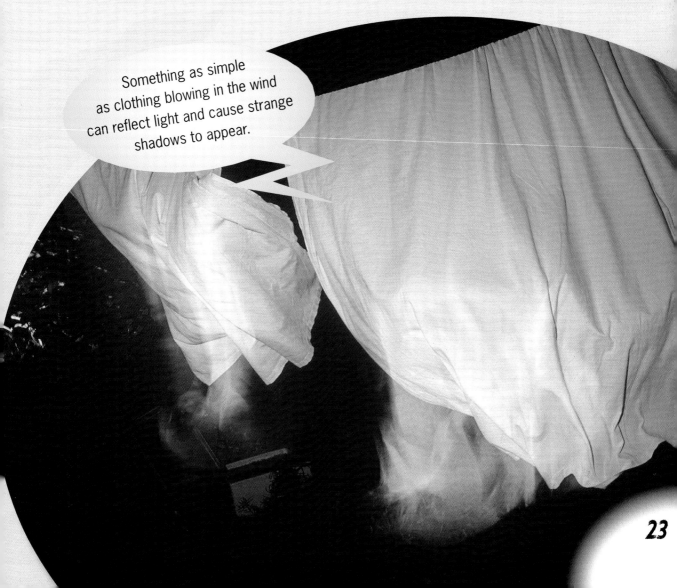

Something as simple as clothing blowing in the wind can reflect light and cause strange shadows to appear.

# HAUNTED HOUSE STAKE-OUT

After investigating a haunting, a **psychic** investigator may want to wait at the site in an attempt to see or hear the ghost for himself or herself. This requires an approach just as scientific as the initial investigation, but more than anything, it requires patience!

## Tools of the trade

Certain pieces of equipment are essential for ghost hunting, and others are useful. Basic tools are a notebook and pens, a torch, a tape measure for making plans of rooms, a tape recorder and a camera. Compact cameras, digital cameras and video cameras are all suitable. The important thing is that a camera can often pick up low-light details that the naked eye cannot.

The trickiest part of ghost hunting is finding the ghosts in the first place before you can photograph them. Investigators use several scientific instruments which show up changes in the conditions in an area which may not be visible to the naked eye. These changes may indicate something peculiar going on, which may be linked to ghostly happenings. Unfortunately, there are still no convincing scientific links between these physical changes and what people see.

Patience can sometimes be rewarded! This photograph, taken in 1974 in a cemetery in Chicago, USA, reveals a mysterious mist.

## Measuring temperature

Psychic investigators often report a drop in temperature during apparent ghostly activity. A simple room thermometer will measure temperature, but a better device is an **infra-red** non-contact thermometer. This detects the strength of infra-red rays coming from an object. All objects give off infra-red rays, and the hotter the object, the more rays it gives off. The non-contact thermometer shows the temperature of anything it is pointed at.

## Magnetic fields

Ghost hunters have also found that ghostly events are often accompanied by a **magnetic field**, just like the magnetic field around an **electromagnet**. So they carry a device called an electromagnetic field (EMF) meter, which measures the strength of the magnetic field it is in.

Thermometers and EMF meters can be electronically linked to a camera so that the camera automatically takes a picture when the temperature or magnetic field changes. This sounds useful, but deciding where to point the camera is a problem because nobody knows where the ghost will appear.

This house in Switzerland has been the scene of many strange happenings: from rattling chains and voices to **apparitions** and moving objects.

# FAKES AND PHOTOS

There is no doubt that some hauntings are faked. There are numerous reasons for claiming to have a ghost in your house. For a start, people like ghosts and ghost stories. If you owned a very old house which was open to the public to visit, imagine how many more visitors you would get if you promised to show them where the ghost of a long-dead, murdered lord is regularly seen! It could be tempting to fake the haunting – after all, nobody could prove you hadn't seen it. Now you can see why owners of old houses, hotels, public houses and restaurants play up stories of ghosts rather than try to keep them quiet. They may even gain publicity by appearing in the local papers, on television and radio. They might even be able to write books to sell. Of course, there is strong competition to claim the 'most haunted house' tag.

Other reasons for fake hauntings include children's pranks to frighten grown-ups on Hallowe'en, to encourage people to go on haunted house guided tours, and even to try to frighten people out of their houses.

## Theatre ghosts

**Many famous theatres are claimed to be haunted, but more interesting is that ghostly figures can appear on stage during plays through trickery. This is done by having a sheet of glass on the stage which reflects the light from a hidden actor.**

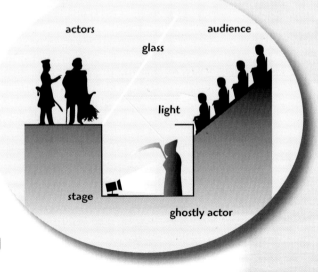

actors

glass

audience

light

stage

ghostly actor

This famous photograph of a ghostly figure was taken at Raynham Hall, Norfolk, England in 1936. It was probably faked by taking two photographs from the same spot.

## Photographs of ghosts

People are most intrigued by spectacular ghosts, such as long-dead knights with clanking armour, or vicious **poltergeists**. Apart from actually seeing the ghost, the best evidence would be a photograph of a ghostly figure or a floating armchair. Fake photographs are easy to put together, especially with modern computer graphics and **digital photography**. There are several old photographs which are claimed to show ghosts, but they were taken by accident rather than on purpose. Close inspection and computer enhancement shows that they are probably multiple photographs, created by two photographs being **superimposed** because the film did not wind on properly.

# WHAT DO YOU THINK?

So can science really solve the mystery of haunted houses? The lack of solid and reliable scientific evidence probably means the answer is "no – not at the moment". Remember that investigators have visited many haunted houses but have found no conclusive proof that ghosts exist. Proving that they don't exist is impossible.

Trick or truth?
This photograph shows a two-year-old boy looking at the ghost of his great-grandmother.

## Do theories about sound, light and moving ground provide any answers?

### Sounds convincing...

- Materials expanding and contracting as they get hotter or colder can cause creaks and bumps, especially in old buildings

- There are lots of old tunnels and mines underground, which can make the ground move causing doors to open by themselves and things to fall off shelves

- Glass in old windows is rarely flat and can cause strange tricks of the light.

### But what about...?

- Ghost stories have existed for thousands of years – can they all be explained by strange sounds in old buildings?

- Psychic investigators have also found strange magnetic fields where ghostly events have been reported

- How can we explain the vivid eyewitness reports of ghosts?

A spooky graveyard above the town of Whitby. Would you go here at night?

There's no doubt that the science of light and sound can explain many odd sights and noises. But, if witnesses are to be believed, and we must assume that they are not all making up or exaggerating their experiences, then there are some hauntings which science cannot explain.

What about the other theories? Do you think any of them might be true? Look at the list of theories below and think about the pros and cons of each. Decide which you think are the most convincing.

- Low **frequency** sounds that are not heard by the human ear can cause people to see things that aren't really there

- **Hallucinations** are a side-effect of diseases like malaria

- Some people have a natural ability to pick up signals from the dead by ESP

- Ghost stories and photos are all fakes.

What are your conclusions? Are there theories you can dismiss without further investigation? Do you have any theories of your own? Perhaps you believe that the spirit lives on after death, in which case ghosts may not seem so strange to you. Try to keep an open mind. Remember that science is constantly evolving and new discoveries are being made all the time. Just because something can't be proved scientifically now, doesn't mean this will always be the case.

# GLOSSARY

**apparition** a visible figure of a person, which is not really the person himself or herself

**county** an area of local government administration in the United Kingdom

**digital photography** photography with a digital camera, which records pictures electronically as data instead of chemically on film. The pictures can be loaded into a computer.

**electromagnet** a magnet made when an electric current flows through a coil of wire

**folklore** the traditional stories and beliefs of a group of people

**frequency** the number of times an event happens. The frequency of a wave is the number of wave crests which pass a point every second.

**friction** a force between two surfaces which tries to stop the surfaces from sliding against each other. The more the surfaces are pressed together, the larger the force of friction is.

**geological** to do with the structure of the Earth or the pattern and types of rocks under the ground

**hallucination** when you think you see or hear something that is not really there

**humidity** the amount of water vapour in the air. The air is very humid on a hot, sticky day.

**infra-red** a type of ray similar to light, but which is invisible to the human eye and carries heat away from where it is made. For example, a fire gives out infra-red rays which you feel as heat on your skin.

**magnetic field** the region around a magnet (or electromagnet) where its magnetic force can be felt

**malicious** with the intention to do harm

**parapsychologist** a person who studies events which cannot be explained by present-day science, such as extra-sensory perception

**poltergeist** a type of ghost which makes noises and moves objects, but is never seen

**psychic** relating to the supernatural

**refracted** light is refracted, or bent, when it passes through different substances, such as water

**retina** the layer of cells at the back of an eye which detects the brightness and colour of the light that hits it and sends messages to the brain

**stately home** a large country house which has normally been the home of the same family for many generations

**subsidence** when underground rocks settle or collapse, making the surface sink downwards. Subsidence can damage buildings.

**superimposed** placed on top of something else

**telekinesis** the apparent movement of objects without anyone or anything touching them

**transparent** see-through, or allowing light to pass through it

**water vapour** the gas form of water, formed when water boils. It is always present in the air.

**wave** a movement in a substance, such as water or air, which passes through the substance, carrying energy with it. For example, a sound wave is made up of a compression travelling through the air.

## Find out more

You can find out more about haunted houses in books and on the Internet. Use a search engine such as www.yahooligans.com to search for information. A search for the words "haunted house" will bring back lots of results, but it may be difficult to find the information you want. Try refining your search to look for some of the people and ideas mentioned in this book, such as "Abraham Lincoln ghost" or "parapsychology".

## More Books to Read

*Out There? Mysterious Visitors*, John Townsend (Heinemann Library, 2004)

*True Ghost Stories*, Paul Dowswell and Tony Allan (Usborne, 2003)

# INDEX